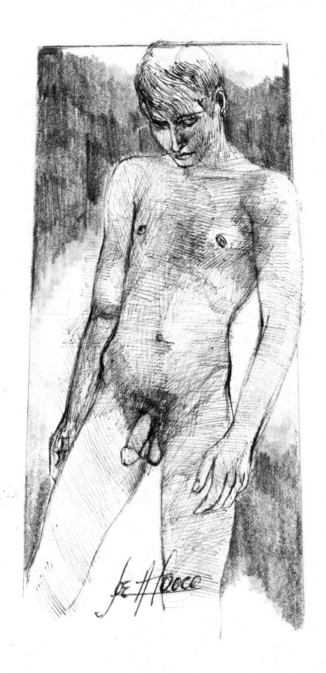

CUTE

and other poems

Jim Everhard

Gay Sunshine Press
San Francisco

Publication of this book was made possible in part by a grant from the National
Endowment for the Arts in Washington, D.C.

Some of these poems have appeared in the following publications:

*Gay Sunshine Journal; Fag Rag; Mouth of the Dragon; Hanging Loose; New: Ameri-
can & Canadian Poetry; Mass Transit; Editor's Choice; Literature and Graphics from
the U.S. Small Press, 1965–1977; Landscapes and Distances: Contemporary Poets
from Virginia.*

Library of Congress Cataloging in Publication Data:

Everhard, Jim, 1946–
    Cute, and other poems.
    I. Title.
PS3555.V36C8 1982   811'.54   82-11704
ISBN 0-917342-92-5 (lim. ed.)
ISBN 0-917342-93-3 (pbk.)

Gay Sunshine Press
PO Box 40397
San Francisco, CA 94140
Write for a complete catalogue of titles.

CONTENTS

I. MEMORIES, DREAMS, DESIRES

II. INNOCENCE

III. CUTE

This book is a flame

for Richard Sawyer

I MEMORIES, DREAMS, DESIRES

In the thousand and thousand embraces
no one can see now
who corrupts and who illuminates . . .

—Mona Van Duyn, from "A Day in Late October"

DAYTON: NON-MEMORIES

for my mother

> It is located in the southwestern
> part of the State, on both banks of
> the Great Miami R., where it receives the
> waters of Mad and Stillwater rivers and
> of Wolf Creek.
> —from *Universal Standard Encyclopedia*, 1

> When Humanity advances, all mothers
> will be isolated before the birth of
> their children in some protected place
> where they shall be surrounded by statues,
> pictures and music.
> —Isadora Duncan, *My Life*, 1927

1.

Born in Dayton, after Hitler,
I was surrounded by precision industry:
cash registers, computing scales,
electric-refrigeration equipment,
automobile parts, paper and
paper-making machinery, filling-
station equipment, lifting jacks,
boilers, fire-fighting equipment,
bicycles, golf clubs, paints
and ice cream cones.

Everyone in Dayton must have a skill.

My mother had no skill
except Catholicism,
and she wasn't even Catholic,
just educated by nuns,
almost a nun herself
until she joined the WAVES.

2.

I have just taken a test that
shows I have no mechanical aptitude.
I took a test in the Navy that
detected effeminate inklings,
because I preferred the ballet
to football. Actually,
football can be quite graceful
in slow motion. Combat, too.
All wars of honor should be fought
in slow motion, each nuance of
fear pin-pointed for viewer absorption.
The ballet is everywhere,
our shadows lie at our feet
like the black tights we
are afraid to pull over our bodies.

3.

I don't remember Dayton.
I would like to remember
the Mad and Stillwater rivers.
No entry for Wolf Creek
in the Universal Standard Encyclopedia.
The Wright Brothers invented
flying in Dayton. What must it
feel like to parachute into water,
into water wrapped in wet silk,
not even hearing the explosion,
to fall into strange water
trying to remember its name?
I'd like to fly over Dayton
in memory of the Wright Brothers.

4.

Flying is graceful because
it is so hard to believe how fast
you are really going. Clouds
slow it all down.

Airplane parts are made in Dayton.
Someday Dayton may become that myth
like Troy or Atlantis.
I'd like to be a part of that myth.
There's a hospital for mental cases
in Dayton. Maybe a man is there,
shell shocked from some past war,
who still thinks flying is impossible.
I would like to talk to him.
I would like to bring him
the wax and feathers
he calls for in the night.
If he is afraid of Mad River,
I will show him Stillwater.
He might think I'm his mother.
That would be all right, too.

5.

When I was pulled from my mother's womb
I vaguely recall a doctor humming,
or maybe it was a nurse
with a tray full of metal objects.
I remember the wings pulled from my back,
discarded with the placenta.
To make me human, perfect.
I was a perfect baby.

6.

When I got my first ten-dollar bill
(for my tenth birthday)
I wanted to buy my mother
everything she missed as a child
during the depression. I wanted to
fly into Dayton and buy her
cash registers, gas pumps,
boilers, bicycles, golf clubs
and ice cream cones.
Instead I gave her
One Hundred and One Favorite Poems.
I liked the way books open, slow, perfect wings.

GIFTS

for my grandmother

I was eight when I got the mumps, on my birthday. When I got sick, Dad would bring me presents, usually games to occupy my time. But this time I wanted paper dolls. I'd played paper dolls all summer with the Weems girls and Linda. One night Dad came home with a bag under his arm. He laid it on my bed and left the room. That was probably the nicest thing he ever did for me. Mom said I'd probably be a famous dress designer. Dad wasn't comforted.

On my tenth birthday my grandparents came bearing gifts. Granddad gave me his coin collection with a book that identified coins and told how much they were worth. Granddad had collected the coins during the war, found them in attics and junk piles. Grandma gave me a plastic jewelry kit. Dad didn't say a word. I made brooches and rings for Mom and Grandma. Grandma said maybe I'd be a famous jewelry designer. Granddad grunted at his son. The coins made my hands smell metallic and the box was too heavy to lug around. I preferred pasting the colored bits of plastic into plastic settings. Grandma wore her pin every time she came to visit. Granddad always asked me how the coin collection was doing, as if it was supposed to do something. I liked the coins that had turned so green with age you couldn't read the dates. Otherwise, it was a pretty dull hobby.

When I turned twelve my grandparents gave me a microscope set. I was so happy I cried and Aunt Audrey cried because she said she had never seen such a grateful child. Everyone thought I'd be a famous biologist. Biology was the only course I ever got an "A" in in high school. I wanted to be a veterinarian. The next year I flunked Chemistry. My last year I wrote a short story for Creative Writing called "Sand Castles Are For Dreamers Only," and Miss May liked it so much she gave me a double "A" on it. It was all about a boy and a girl after a beach party. The girl is drunk and tries to make the boy jealous. She builds a sand castle. She's horny. The boy finally kicks over the sand castle, she runs into the sea and he catches her and kisses her and she sees that her castle was only sand. Linda Buddenhagen, the most popular girl in the school, said it was beautiful. She was really into the Beach Boys and surfing movies. She always said, "Bust your buns," when she liked you. After that I decided to become a famous writer. I was too old for gifts and people started giving me money. I refused the third prize award in the school literary contest because Sartre had just refused the Nobel Prize. Everyone thought I was going to be a famous writer. They wanted me to use the money for dates, to get my nose out of books.

THE INVISIBLE BROTHER

for John

I am reading.

Albert, my brother, storms into the house,
slams his pitcher's mitt on the floor
and calls me a "jerk off!"

He calls me this because
everyone knows I am a sissy
and I hate sports.

I say, "I don't know what you mean."

He calls me a pansy, a faggot,
        an ivory tower intellectual.

I get this intuition: "Did you
        lose the ball game?"
Albert always thought Dad blamed
        him when the team lost.

He reaches for my throat.
The book floats out of my hands.
It is a picture book about animals.
My heart is suddenly hot,
like a brush fire sweeping
across the savanna.

"My heart is weak," I lie,
my passive way of surviving,
        as if he shouldn't be strangling me.

As I am being strangled
Dad enters with his box that hisses.

He is completely naked
except for a full body tattoo
of a coach's uniform.
When he's disgruntled
he brings out his box that hisses.
It sounds like a punctured tire
or a witch doctor's rattle.

Albert now has a death grip on me.

Dad looks up,
shouts at me not to play so loud,
to shut up or go outside.
Then he leans over and
listens to his box.

I look around
but do not see Albert.
I only feel this
hot constriction
around my throat
that is, at once,
violent and tender,
distant and close,
and I am not sure now
whose hands they are,
or if they are hands at all.

FOR MARCIE

the last night
you came to the house
had pizza and
after an uneasiness
that wasn't going to end
I told you I was no
lover boy remembering
what Warren Beatty had said
somewhat unconvincingly
to Faye Dunaway but
remembering also how things
never ran smoothly with us
the night you called me
and confessed you'd
taken more speed
after I tried unsuccessfully
to break it up but
was still having trouble
with my male ego
our first time together
in bed   I pounced on you
kissing feeling knowing
if it didn't work out
I could excuse it for being
the first time and all
but later, again . . .
and you asked about my fantasies
to try and help   I couldn't
tell you they were all with men
we decided not to rush things
I knowing they would come
to a dead halt . . .
the first night
afterwards not sleeping
but both of us pretending,

you in my arms
a cat on the windowsill
your room mate and another man
in the next room in the
quiet of that house,
a fog creeping across the orchard
into which morning birds
disappeared one by one

SAILOR

No one ever asked me.
I got all the way through the Navy
without so much as a proposition.
I remember going to bed waiting
so I could touch his head
with my bare feet. Finally, he looked
at me strange but never said a word.
He thought I was asleep.
My friends were mostly married and
we got drunk together but
no one expected me to pick up girls.
I read books like Dostoievski and
Thomas Hardy. Our ship never left
the East Coast. I never experienced
exotic fruit. Once Henry and I
got so drunk we couldn't find
the ship and he proposed to an elderly
woman on his knees while she told
stories about her son in Vietnam.
I looked like him.
Her husband bought us enough drinks
we got so fucked up but
I never touched Henry
and no one ever thought I did.
I guess I wasn't sexy being scared.

SOUTH YUMA RIVER, SUMMER 1971

for Harry Lehman III

I remember catching you
eating cold bean sprouts
from the evening's meal
before you thumbed to work.
I was still a little drunk
from the "green death" we'd
finished off on the roof.
That day we'd ride bikes
to your mother's and you'd
thrash into her pool
the rest of us watching hesitant
as you finally emerged
like a new thing,
unable to speak.

It was the same
in the orchard near South Yuma River.
You went down alone
with a bottle of wine
after a day of mending branches.
That night you brought back
the crazy French Canadians and
drove the pick-up to a bar
fifty miles away to raise hell.

I couldn't tell you I loved you
until now, living with these
images after two years
and still too close to them
to make sense of my fear.
You wanted to become a legend,
I wanted one poem that could
capture the joy you expressed
naked in the mountain water
expounding on clean living
as you tied your clothes to shore
to wash them,
let the river run through them.

DISTANCE

for Walt Senterfitt

I don't want to change anything
with my poetry   I just want
to touch something like
it's never been touched before

my hands come out to you
because the birds
that are my fingers
sense the sky there
that they can open there

I taste you
the way the birds taste
the sky   flying through it
as the Buddha tastes the cloud
tasting himself

taste with my fingers

my eyes

my cock

my tongue

into these flow the feelings
that the words come from
through the touch
that is us
surrounded by distance

the distance we have come
the distance we must go

KNOTS

for Martha, Lee and, especially Diane

in the city I take a taxi
to visit my love who waits
with dinner on the stove
in a warm room.
                    Diane,
my housemate, who's coming off
a nervous breakdown, wants more
love. I, who sometimes feel unloved,
am beginning to wonder about
my own senses,
whether or not I can hold that
balance between desire
and reality. Actually, Michael,
my lover, is already married.

We meet at the cafeteria
in the University where I work.
Michael is glib and I,
as usual, expectant.
The table hunches between us.
He relates quite well
with my friend, Bill,
another quick wit.
                    I am
surrounded
            by other,
older friends.
                No,
that was the birthday party.
Sam brought me
a candle shaped like a mouse.
We can be any shape we want to be.
Rich brought me a monogrammed stein.
Walt gave me a piggy-back plant

and a cake with twenty-nine
candles I'd hoped to avoid. But
I needed that sentimental
gesture because my lover and I
were not working it out and
Diane was already beginning
to act strangely, disconnectedly.
Paranoia frightens me.
She feels I have withdrawn
and I have but her persistent
reassurances that the situation
is all right do not comfort me
because Michael and Sam
are talking quietly, intimately,
and I am resenting myself
for feeling jealous of Sam.

Walt kisses me knowing
it can't be as before
when we were lovers. Once,
in the car, Diane told me
she fantasized we were lovers
Michael said, risk it with me,
and I did.
        I want love.
        All love is risk.
I care about Michael, Walt,
Diane, Lee, Sam, Bill, Herb,
Rick. I even imagine I care
about Jane, Michael's wife,
though we've never met and
when I am depressed about Michael
I play voodoo and stick pins
in an imaginary heart. This
frightens me because it is my heart,
filled with pins,
a doll shaped like myself.

* * *

Now Diane suspects me and
stares at me for long moments
afraid I'm poisoning her and
Michael tells me not to guilt-trip
myself. Walt listens
patiently for a crack in the knot
that will burst it open. In
one hysterical moment
when my head is muddled
but my heart is clear
and deep, I chased Michael
across H Street
calling him a fucking coward
in broad daylight. I
didn't care who saw us.
Running is the only way I can
keep up with him and
I feel like I'm heading for
the same collision he hopes
will stop everything in
one instant moment of
recognition.

He sings he will survive.

Diane complains of pains
in her stomach and
brings a knife down to
house meeting to protect herself.
Ray calls the police while
Lee and I try to talk, to calm down.

Diane dances in the flowers
cutting them with her knife
The knife sings a simple song.
The knots fall like petals and

in the city I take a taxi
to visit my love who waits
with dinner on the stove
in a warm room.

MEMORY OF ROANOKE

for Tom

I am still haunted
by the memory of that knock
on the door after we had
already undressed and touched,
and of the boy waiting
outside when you opened it.
Later you told me some guys
in the bar sent boys
to knock on your door at night.
These boys would make love to you,
then report something
to these guys who
couldn't seem to learn enough about you.
You are the quiet sort.
Only some of these boys
would return and tell you
not to give them away,
and they would stay the whole night.
To you it meant nothing, you said.
You could hardly see their faces
in the dark,
for they always came after dark
and you could not turn on your porch light.
This was, after all, a Southern town.
They came. You invited them in.
And afterwards you would sleep
in the warm spot on the sheets
like a ghost.
I knew then how easily
your heart could be broken.

REASONS WHY I LOVE YOU

for Richard

You read the classics,
are a clean cut loner
and, as a boy, sang in
the Episcopal choir.

Your mother sings ner-
vously to strangers on the
telephone. I make you ner-
vous. We like the same

movies. You are too
frightened not to be
gentle. You have courage
without flaunting it.

You always tell the truth
and expect me to. You
read my poetry nervous-
ly. You tell me about

all the people you'd
like to murder some day
and I believe you knowing
even the things that

bug me about you
contribute to a lasting
impression. I know you.
I like your butch bitch-

iness. I want to touch
you touching me. It's true:
we look alike except for
your premature balding spot.

I like you lying on your
right side with my chest
against your back, my arms
around under your arms

so that my hands touch
and curve around your breasts,
your smooth shoulders and
my cock presses into your ass.

When I talk to you you
listen and sometimes cry
or laugh or get a hard on.
When you respond to me

I respond to you. When
I spread my legs apart,
you fit perfectly between them;
I could fall asleep

flying like this.
You are my parachute,
my bumpy-grindy night,
the grasshopper of

my conscience. I love
trying to convince you
that I love you knowing
you are not yet ready

because I make you nervous.
I like it when you tell me
you are afraid because I
love you too much you

are afraid of my love
which you want the way
you want it when you
want it and are glad

I won't give it to you
solely on your terms,
Your abounding sense of
chaos steadies my hand

for your body gives shape
to the love I feel,
the way you move me
to desire your desire.

AFTER SLEEP

for one night stands

waiting
for your eyes
to open

to see you
remember me
the first time

ENEMY

for Richard

"*enemy is not a word of hate. It's what we call
our lovers when we don't love them any more
now they've rejected us.*"

—Ron Schreiber

I hadn't been
rejected
for so long
I'd forgotten
it could happen
           to anybody
but when you
came up the elevator
so serious
and said we should
talk about
what we were doing
           together,
well, I thought
we knew
and I already knew
how shabbily I had
treated you
         lately
thinking: I'll get over it
whatever "it" was
and treat you better
not counting on you
not being around.

For a month
we didn't talk,
then when I ran
into you we'd
go home, spend
a weekend together

until you told me
it's okay
while we're together
but the rest of the week
you're angry
                    so you
tell me
don't write any more cards,
don't call,
I can't see you,
                    let's play dead
unto each other.

And when I saw you
with another man
I had two enemies,
one serious, one mock,
I even asked him
in a bar: What's your name?

Ed

Aren't there tribes
believe when you
know a man's name
you have power over him?

I have no power,
write on your mailbox:

        Forgive me
        I'm gone

I've gone crazy like Electra
in the cartoons,
want to slay our children,
throw a shirt you gave me
for Christmas down the
toilet instead and
spend two weeks with
a toilet that won't flush.

I must be the crazed,
destructive, oc-
tagonal, furious one,
the one the rational,
cool, decisive one avoids,
the one
        who projects
while you protect
        yourself
                from projectiles.

I begin to believe
life is superficial,
surfaces, what you see
is all you get, decide

to murder him
(which interests
my shrink who
thinks I am
suicidal),

shoot, but I don't have a gun,
think I could aim one
                at his heart
        but people who shoot their lover
always look miserable,
        poison, push off cliff, strafe,
ackack attack, hit man, roll over
        tractor, smack, insult, maim,

        stone   crack   skull

                * * *

and other baroque possibilities:

        1. Fatal crab attack
        2. Hole punch
        3. Heavy on the mayo

4. The Force
5. Hide the cheese slicer
6. Vegamatic
7. Tiny time capsules
8. Body odor bombs

Still, I prefer:

stone

crack

skull

exhausted by
dreams of torture,
ineffectual,

I want to change reality,
go to gym, work out,
hate work, become
moody typist who can
only type a little slow,
has to hunch over desk,
scribble on index cards
suicide notes for all my enemies,
take hour and half lunch,
grow, burst out
in tears for no apparent
reason, become diarrhetic,
my body getting it all out,
for stupid little shit,
pump iron, bench press,
sweat on his photograph,
leg curl, quit smoking
but not steaming,
eat more, change my name,
prepare for my enemy.
my lover whose face
I remember as if
written in stars.

Isn't the name "Ed" in
the word "dead" if you
spell it backwards?

"No, I'm not
in love," he says,
"I'm just the kind
of guy who has to
see someone regular."
He's the kind of guy
who called us
whores, etc.

We are enemies
who must share
the same territory.
I even asked him
in a bar,
"Why don't you move?"
and he said, "You
came up to me." I replied,
"I don't mean here,
in the bar, I mean
why don't you move
out of town?" He moved

across the bar.
If there's anything wrong
to say, leave it to me
to say it. I used to think
it was because I'm a Sagittarius,
now I know it's because
I pick up phone,
dial his number,
the minute I hear
his voice, I hang up.
I want to talk to him,
yet I want to torture him
also so he'll feel
as anxietous as me.

I hang up and feel
guilty knowing he
feels angry and
doesn't talk to me
about anything.

Aren't we oppressed
enough not to oppress
each other? I leave
my note and mean it,
forgive me,
I'm gone.

I have burnt your
village to the ground,
uprooted your corn,
stampeded your ponies,
and still you insist
you will survive
without me,

as if we were separable.

We are.

II INNOCENCE

for Tom Nolan

this we were, this is how we tried to love,
and these are the forces they had ranged against us,
and these are the forces we had ranged within us,
within us and against us, against us and within us

—Adrienne Rich, from XVII of "Twenty-Four Love Poems"

1. YOU CAN'T FUCK WITH
MOTHER NATURE

I kneel down at Blake's feet
and dig with my fingernails
until I have a hole maybe
an inch and a half wide
and seven inches deep.
Blake rubs his crotch
casually in my face
so as not to attract attention
and I pull down my fly
and stick my cock into the earth,
and begin fucking
and fucking
and fucking
waiting for a cop to come by and
ask me what I'm doing.
I'm sorry officer,
but I was horny
and the earth looked so,
I don't know,
beautiful
today I just got this overwhelming inspiration
like Scarlett O'Hara.
You've seen GWTW, haven't you officer?
where she kneels down
at the intermission
and eats dirt.
Well, I'd call that rimming
and she did it on the silver screen
for everyone to see.
She got an Academy Award.
I haven't such gigantic aspirations
to exhibit myself like she did
but I've always been horny
for days now and
well,
look at it this way,

the earth was here
and so was I
and like Steven Stills says,
if you can't love the one you love,
then love the one you're with.
What are you going to arrest me for anyway,
fucking with the earth?
Maybe you ought to get some of those
fucking Industrialists
who are poisoning everybody.
Cum's biodegradable, I think.
If not, I may have some problems
shitting in a few years
since I usually take it
all the way
up my ass.
I'm not into fucking that much
and I'm probably afraid of women,
but it's a beautiful day
and I wanted to fuck Mom so bad
and I just want to have a good time
but Dad would beat the shit
out of me
it's coming out of me
and Mom doesn't like fucking anyhow.

The officer doesn't find anything innocent about it.
He pierces me with his fuck eyes
and I come
to the little country church in the vale
come to
consciousness again
transcend the moment
get into the badge,
and he grabs me and Blake,
whisks us down to the station
in the vale,
valley of,
massive, impressive butch shadows.

Death is butch.
I want to sing railroad songs
but Blake says, "Shut up,
shut up, fuck head,"
while they frisk us a couple of times
though I insist the only gun I own
is empty. I request that the arresting officer
frisk me again,
check out my ass hole, buddy.
I even promise
to pay child support for the child
if I've accidentally impregnated the whole fucking earth
like one of those sci-fi epics
about devil seed and demon lust and voodoo
and flying saucers
with sperm valves and ugliness
and big styrofoam boobs.

II. MOMMA'S VISION

I'm afraid of hard work.
My momma never made me empty the trash.
She let me help fold clothes instead.
I want the revolution to happen
without me. I don't know what to do.
What words are powerful?
I'm afraid, I can't imagine
a homosexual army
unless we find a tough lesbian
to be general. We really are
delicate people. The wrong kind of look
sends us fleeing into the streets.
We're still afraid, all too often
to hold each other. I still hear friends say
this one's too fem, that one's too butch,
this one's too arrogant, that one's too needy.

We float through one night
and another night,
on and on wherever desire carries us,
like pollen in the wind,
and arrive like sand in my shoes,
at the discos and porno shops
and gay liberation meetings.
Everyone tells me
the times have already changed,
Carol Burnett's more popular
than Anita Bryant.
We should be loose,
forget politics
unless there's a gay or pro-gay candidate
carrying the banner of
Smiley Capitalism.
Cash in.
Watch tv.
Go to the movies.
Buy twenty-dollar tickets to
a benefit for faggots at the Kennedy Center,
très posh.
Faggots rot in jail after the revolution.
The October League will eat you up.
But I still have friends
who write songs
with the word "she" in them.
I still know people
who are fired from jobs
because they are faggots.
I know people who can't quite
make it
all
hang
together.
I still can't,
quite.
Remember, it's usually your daddy
telling you you got to be realistic,
Rea-ah-Lis-Tic

toe the line,
get educated,
get a job,
join the forces of Capitalism.
And your momma still
listens to your dreams
and wants you to be happy.
Someone wants you to be happy,
right, but she can't help,
can only hold onto you
like you're the misunderstood martyr
and she's the Virgin Mary
and Joseph just sort of disappears
into the background,
(the quickest way
to kill your father
is to omit him from the story),
of those two amazing stories.
But she doesn't understand really
or keep from hurting
and hides from her own inability to understand
why you insist on being different,
fucked up, crazy,
not really her son at all,
but a man as strange to her
as her husband.
Mom doesn't understand anything
anymore, she only knows
it came from her body
and she must love it,
must love something
because her body was huge
with something inside it
and now it is empty
and nothing will ever grow inside her again.
She will never be clean,
never innocent.
She lost her innocence
when you killed it
taking a turn no one could conceive possible.
You slew her child.

III. POPPA'S VISION

When I come out into the streets
I bring out the whole family,
an old time reunion in one body,
a picnic of heart and bone and guts
that no one wants to eat.
Blake buys me a button
shaped like a tombstone:
> THE NUCLEAR FAMILY EXPLODED
> BEFORE THE BOMB DID.
Now the Fathers are gathering
in their uniforms
and the Mothers are busy
dressing and undressing the babies,
quietly muttering to themselves
all the confusion
of the family tree
every branch stripped and brittle
except for the very top ones
whipping about in their mouths
(going down on Hubby)
till their tongues bleed
and the babies squawk
for the garbled words
they will never learn.
"I remember yesterday," Blake says,
now a little stoned,
"but I can't remember my mother's face,
only a peculiar twist of flesh,
and a grunt
like when I first found Daddy
fucking Mommy
and she was under him
grunting
and he wasn't making a sound
as if his voice
was lost in his hands

holding onto her small breasts
the way he gripped
the straps in the subway
going under the city
to a job
that was like a foreign country."
I told Blake I fantasized
that my Dad was a spy
for Russia and
he traded top secrets
for women
whose names he couldn't even pronounce.
But I knew Mom was innocent
and I knew I was evil
for filling in all the missing
spaces in Daddy's life.
Now I don't even call him.
I told him I was a faggot
and a huge silence
like an ice age
fell between us.
I don't need him,
he only needed me
to see how I would develop.
But that's the kind of innocence
that kills a child,
and I've been looking for a father
for a long time now.
My father comes back to me
in a policeman's uniform,
motivated no longer by love of me
but by pride of nation
and as a representative
of banks and corporations
and stockholders of tomorrow.
He tells Blake and me
we can't dance in the street
if we hold onto each other.

All two men have to do
is stand face to face
and if they don't try to kill each other
or make each other invisible,
zap,
they must be queers.
The fathers are not innocent.
They know who they want dead.
Yet my words
have turned my father to stone
and like an ancient idol
with a curse
he falls over in the earthquake
and crushes those who believe
too sincerely in his silence
and call it his strength.

IV. DON'T LOOK BACK

There was no revolution
at Woodstock.
It sold records
but didn't change
the relationships of production
and it ain't made my life
any easier either.
When I listen to the record
it speaks to me
like a history book.
That's where my head was back then.
Even here the words are dead.
Blake went to Woodstock
where a language
was born and died
in Altamont.

"I got some cock there,
but it reinforced my already
abounding sense
of Woody Allenitis," he said.
"sometimes I almost wish
I was in jail
so I could sing those angry blues,
(which, materialistically, were blacks),
but it's easier to think
the revolution has already come and gone.
We still have the music,
don't we? I got my stereo,
(m-y-s-t-e-r-e-o!)
and my dope
and sex
and dead voices on celluloid.
Like a string of pearls
somebody killed for
and found they weren't pearls at all,
(probably petroleum products instead).
All that's dead in me now,
like a child
who never saw
the light of day."
I have never seen Blake
this resigned
but I know he doesn't like that word.
So I don't use it.
"All I know anymore
are the names of the people
I love," I say,
"and even those change.
We end up runnning away from each other.
They abandon me
Like Daddy did.
What's left to hold us together?"
"My heart breaks
when I am with you,"
Blake says, "because I'm afraid
I have invented you
out of my own needs."

V. COMING

Nervously my fingers
unbutton his shirt,
as if I half expect
to find a picture of my father
tattooed to his chest.
His nipples are tiny roses
and when I touch them
they rise like birds
into the holy air.
His hands explore my back
softly. They feel like
my own wings fluttering
and I know I am going up,
growing up as if I were a child
realizing he is no longer
a child. Only these simple,
delicate images,
roses, birds, child,
come to mind,
as if my mind belonged
not to myself now
but to an angel.
I know this is not
the revolution,
only a miniscule
giving and taking
and that it will end
almost without history,
in time, even as his lips
nibble at my nipples
as if they were candy
ready to melt in his mouth.
How many times men
have nibbled away at me
until I was unable to rise,
unable to button my shirt,
unable to speak.

Yet this time I feel
all will remain
or return,
and something else be left,
maybe only a small consolation,
a single hippie
alone in a field
smelling a flower.

We touch the ground.
He rolls on top of me,
leaves sticking to his back
like many small wings.
Our bodies are changing
into little Charlie Chaplins,
and the world becomes a warm gold rush.
We are hungry
and we feed each other
like a mother feeds her child
from her own nipple
not because he is her child
but because he is a child
and he's crying from hunger
and she has something for him
that has grown in her own body
out of love and it must be given.

We are naked
as our cocks touch
and our bodies tremble.
They could be feminine bodies
or animal bodies
or the wings of a dragonfly
or fire in the dark center
of a lump of coal.
Words, images, race through my mind,
rose, bird, child, angel,
lips, nipples, world, star,
gold, mother, cock, love,
dragonfly, fire, coal,
come, coming, coming out

and out and out
until I am totally in light,
in the sun,
in the eyes of everyone,
naked,
vulnerable,
in a fearful ecstasy
that multiplies
like loaves of bread and fishes,
and the more I give
the less hungry I become
weeping light,
holding on,
letting go,
kicking free,
opening up,
my hands reaching out
stretching
grasping
like a baby's hands
pulling in
like the wings of a bird,
surrounded by sky,
like a cock,
sliding into my mouth,
shaped like a thumb,
sliding into my asshole,
wings expanding,
mind outside,
inside,
"Where is the Revolution?"
I want to cry out
but there are no words
and time has escaped
or we have escaped from time,

and his legs
glide slowly
over my legs.
Our feet touch ground
in each other,

like walking over a mirror
that is not a mirror
but a discovery,
a new world
of self and selflessness
where I touch myself,
the stranger,
through his hands,
his chest,
his tongue and lips,
his cock,
his ass,
and I do not know how we got here
or why we are here,
except to meet the stranger,
learn of this presence,
the substantial shadow,
the constant companion,
the friend,
the enemy,
the father and mother,
the brother and sister,
the child
who only wants to hide
in love
and forget the world.

We kiss
as if kisses were words,
rose, bird, child, angel,
lips, nipples, world, star,
gold, mother, cock, love,
dragonfly, fire, coal,
core, light, sun, bread,
fishes, hands, sky, thumb,
asshole, revolution, time,
touch, mirror, stranger, shadow,
companion, friend, enemy,
father, mother, sister, brother,
hide, love, forget, world.

My mouth is empty.
We lie apart,
each of us trying to remember
our own name,
knowing each moment
we must begin again,
that we will not laugh
at yesterday's jokes
or believe in last year's revolution
or ever again be able
to touch the cunt of our mother
or swim through the sea
of our father's cum.

Like fish spit up on the shore
we multiply only
in the eyes of others
and live only
in the hands of those
who would help us back into the sea
where, for a moment,
before we are spit out again,
we will not have to struggle,
surrounded by love,
surrendering to our own joy.
Yet over the beach
the suffused cries of suffering
and anger
continue to rise like mist,
and from the mist
words begin to form again,
new words
pointing back to the world,
a new word,
for innocence,
a grunt,
confused somewhere between
life and death.

III CUTE

"Even laughter may yet have a future."

—Nietzsche, from *The Gay Science*

MONOLOGUE FOR AN AGING QUEEN

(in homage to T. S. Eliot's possible homosexuality)

O!O!O! that Shakespearean drag!
I must rush out as I am, and walk the street
with my hair down. O! Miss Veronica Lake!

O violet hour when sailors drift home,
I shall show you glitter in a handful of
rhinestones. They call to me, "Hiya, Cynth!"

Unreal city, bring home the boys
under your neon fog. Madame So-So's
in love once more with a funky Phoenician.

Going down a fortnight into his seaweed,
rocking in his rumba bones, yielding
to his whirlpools. A good night for drowning,

good night, indeed, for my greying poet
with paling headaches and one coy mistress
in the golden boas of my ennui shoulders.

Give me a peach! Give me the cock
on the roof tree! The grass is singing
Shakespearean ragtime. To be, to be!

ANYTHING BUT MURDER

I love him.
I hate him.
I love him.
I hate him.
He's a little more fem
than I usually prefer
but I like him.
He's too butch
with all those levis
and the dog whistle
on the choke chain,
but I could learn
to appreciate him:
after all, he's Harvard, Class
of 69. Well, if it's not
love, it's not mutual aversion either.
Except for the fact he hustles
I would marry him
if he asked me
at Dignity. I don't expect
anything but I wouldn't mind
if he asked me to the G.A.A. Dance.
I don't usually cook this kind of meal,
but this pheasant flew
through my window and
ruined the spaghetti sauce.
We'd have it under glass
if I didn't just buy
a whole new set of tupperware at the office.
Oral sex doesn't usually turn me on much,
but I kind of like the way his lips
circle around the words with
the long o's in them.
I didn't even notice him
until he asked me if I wanted to get high.

It was five minutes to three
and we'd ignored each other
all night but then he did
this irresistible thing
that really turned me on,
and I didn't think there was enough of me left
to be turned on,
but I beamed up for six plush minutes.
Then we said goodbye
and exchanged numbers
in case either of us
discovered symptoms.
And he gave me the phone number
to this pay booth
in the bus station.
Then I knew he didn't really care.
It was an effect from the poppers.
Half his brains had been blown away,
the half where his phone number was stored.
Only five of the seven digits were off.
Four and a half. I misread one.
We didn't talk about a meaningful relationship
until after our first play
together at the Kennedy Center.
The idea of adopting a gay foster child
didn't turn him on
but it has always been my dream.
I guess there's a little mother
(someone once called me "leedle motha")
inside me.
He won't give me back the ring.
I didn't want a used one anyway.
I was serious when I called him a hot number.
I told him I never went home with anyone the
first night
but that I have this yacht
that we could sail
down to Rio
if he's serious
about wanting a meaningful relationship.

But he told me he was forty.
I thought you were nineteen or twenty.
I don't like to be cornered by anyone
without a drink in one hand
and the keys to a new XKE in my other.
I only asked for bus fare home.
I'm in town,
just visiting,
so let's make a romantic evening of it
and never see each other again.
Don't look back.
If I could only find the words.
If you'd only shut up.
I don't care how many trophies you won
for high school wrestling.
Diana Ross is the best singer in the world.
Barbra Streisand is a better actress.
Judy Garland has more sentimental appeal.
Marlene Dietrich is intellectual.
So, your wife lets you out on weekends.
Any Wednesday.
Any weekend.
After basketball practice.
Any time, any place, anything.
Not tonight.
I have a headache.
I had a lousy day at work
and tomorrow starts too damn early.
Maybe,
But we have to go to your place
or my lover, who is insanely jealous,
might try to put you
in your place, removed, silenced;
he thinks I'm in Seattle
at the Young Socialists' Convention.
My parents might have you arrested.
He was okay.
He was a ten.
He was seven.
He was a zero.

He fell asleep
after I blew him.
He's so boring
he doesn't make waves
on an electrocardiogram.
I thought he was pretty hot
until I kissed the needle marks.
I still can't remember his name.
He just wanted a place to crash.
Ten weeks later.
He's a refugee from a halfway house.
You can't judge a man by his cologne.
He made me listen to every record
Phil Spector ever had anything to do with,
Do-ron-ron.
Four days later I developed this incredible sore throat.
Six days later I had a drip.
Eleven days later the chancre appeared.
Two weeks later I woke up with
this fierce, burning itch all over me.
Then the warts popped out.
Two months later my eyeballs turned yellow.
I'm catching up on all the rest
I've missed since I came out.
I'm looking for an alternative
to the bar scene.
By the time I find a lover
I'll be too old to get it up.
My friends say it's just growing pains.
Have you considered the baths? The movies?
I just want to see a good, old fashioned movie.
I want to stay home.
I want to go out.
I want to stay home.
I want to go out.

LOOKING FOR THE LUMBERJACK

I need someone
to chop down my trees,
someone in red flannel
and denim,
black hair, a moustache,
and maybe a beard,
and deer eyes
quick, vulnerable.
I am looking for the man
who ran into the forest
and never came back.
With my lips
I will remove the pine needles
from his chest.
I am searching for the man
who is alone,
not because he doesn't feel
he needs anyone,
but because, for all his manhood,
he couldn't give up
the sadness and love
he felt and,
rather than do that,
chose to live with himself.
I am waiting for his return.
he will return,
quiet, austere and gentle,
a man who cuts down trees
for firewood
and smears his lips
with berries
and dances in the rain.
I want a man
who is willing
to live with himself,
a man who will tell me
I must live with myself.

"What Captures Light Belongs To What It Captures"
—Thom Gunn

your hair
is not the most beautiful
hair in the world
in fact   it's a little bit
scruffy   an early and
well concealed balding spot
only visible to the
tuned-in eye
the eye that belabors
hesitates
even trembles at times
as it rests upon you
because the light
comes from your hair
blonde and brown
not really like honey
but honey-like
your beautiful light
that opens my eyes
just a little wider
I am as much captive
of your imperfections
as I am
by the way
you perfect me

CRUISING

I feel sure-footed,
yet nervous,
like the tightrope walker
who has made
that walk
a hundred times
and never stumbled,
whose life is filled
with falling.

I could do it blindfolded,
deaf,
without wit
or that taut feeling
that digs into my feet.

I may have heard
these people talking
in a dream once, many times,
the ones who meet
at the edge of light,

Or maybe it was a questionnaire
I've filled out again and again,
Who? What? Why? When? How?
What a strange custom.
What a strange way
to get to know the world,
like the delicate whiskers
on a panther's nose.

BLONDES AND BRUNETTES

The blondes come from cold countries
where they lived on Viking ships
for many generations and discovered
America before the Mediterranean
brunette, Christopher Columbus.
Blondes are always the first to arrive
so they can primp in the mirror.
Brunettes languor, do not bathe as often
and live in apartments that look like
they've been lived in. Brunettes
generally come from southern countries
where the sun has pigmented their skin
so they always look healthy and robust
while blondes always look a little pale,
even undernourished. Blonde babies are
abandoned before brunette babies
because they are prissier. Their blue eyes
always look more prophetic than brunettes
who always look a little sleepy,
even when they're the ones doing the talking
which is most of the time since blondes
pinch their lips. Brunettes are hit men
and blondes are targets. But blondes
are called bombshells and
brunettes aren't called anything unless they have
a little red mixed in in which case
they may be referred to as fireballs.
Blondes get asked to dance more than brunettes.
But brunettes have more rhythm. Blondes
get pregnant faster than brunettes but
are better at keeping it a secret.
Blondes prefer seafood while brunettes like
tacos and hot sauce. Some brunettes are
so light brown they could pass for blondes
and do whenever they can. A blonde would never

pass for anyone other than those he is already
posing as. Blondes gain more prestige for less
effort than brunettes. But brunettes are manly,
they don't care. They know they could have
a blonde under their thumb whenever they want
because opposites attract and brunettes make
more money than blondes so they can support them.
Blondes, on the other hand, make better movies,
their blonde hair burnished by the eye of the camera
as if they were haloed, for blondes are angels
who have forgotten they are angels. Brunettes
are more intelligent, however, and exult in
the essence of the absence of aura, as if they had
created the world. Blondes are more religious
but never penitent. Brunettes are haunted by guilt,
often tortured by the past, the one thing they aren't
very intelligent about. Blondes are superficial.
Brunettes are potent. Blondes are fragile. Brunettes
are unable to see entirely through a blonde.
Blondes are plush. Brunettes are crass.
Blondes fool around more. Brunettes get caught
less because their eyes are so sincere
a blonde never wants to doubt the brunette.
The blonde thinks quietly to himself for a long time
and is accused of ignoring his brunette lover.
A brunette goes gray but the blonde is still blonde.
Yet the blonde has bad joints. The brunette is always
stronger so he can lift the blonde into bed.
The blonde dies first because the brunette is a better
mourner and old men are supposed to be stooped and gray
and wiser. And when the blonde dies,
he remembers he was an angel
and he lies underneath the eyelids
of the old man and shows him the way to heaven.

MYSTERIES OF THE HEART

for Ed Cox

Make your hands
into fists and
hold your fists
together. This
is the size of
your heart, not
smaller or larger.

Slowly open your
fists until your
hands are cupped
as if to hold
something delicate
with careful joy,
something that breathes.

Spread your hands
further open until
they are flat like
opened wings. Imagine
the body that
joins them together,
the heart at its center.

Let your hands
fall apart and
down to your sides
while you breathe in
and out, like the motion
of a wing, a life
of flight, of falling.

Imagine only your
hands exist
and the air.

Your body is air.
Only your hands
keep falling down
through the air.

They continue
to fall until
somehow they become
grounded in heart,
in the radiant
coherence of heart
in shadow.

The heart has
no eyes. The heart
has no ears. The
heart has no tongue
or fingers or wings.
Like a machine
it labors and

breaks down.
The lights go out.
No one comes close
anymore. The heart
is turned off by
its own exhaustion.
In the dark where

it was born
the heart dies
without escape,
without light,
without answers
in the mystery
of the hands

that have fallen away.

ODE TO THE DUCHESS LA BLAH

for Gary

I.

The whole world is a stage,
especially DuPont Circle,
a swan lake of second-class gunmen,
junkies and glassy-eyed housewives,
artistes and us. Tricks
roost on the fountain's edge,
finger the water.
     You shine
100% swank
in your Italian straw hat,
cranberry scarf and
Goodwill sweater,
(you swore Sonja Henie wore it in *Iceland*).
You are the only person I know
who claims to have made it with
all four of the Marx Brothers. Only you
get a hard on watching
Duck Soup.
You are the only drag queen ever
to willfully imitate Kitty Carlisle.
Cocking a gander you said,
"I sing America swishing," in your
best imitation of Walt "the troub.,"
(short for troubador) Whitman.
       No man
is ugly, all are your "little Colonne,
little cabbage." A motorcycle
rumbles round and round playing our song.

2.

In the park alone, reading *My Life,*
I await archangel Esenin,
Andy Warhol, Duke Mantee, the Flying Leathernecks,
you. I feel like June Allyson
in the "optimistic cinema."
   On page 255 I read:

>   "Yes," I continually cry, "let me
>   be Pagan, be Pagan!" but I was probably
>   never much more advanced than to be
>   a Pagan Puritan, or a Puritanical Pagan.

Winter makes puritans of us all.
We scrape by on the remains of
past revolutions, warm our hands
with the names of old flames.

The fountain is closed.
Leaves swarm down like left-over
paratroopers from a John Wayne war epic.
Round the circle they are blown
with a kind of grace,
a leaf scarf flying in the wind.
You pulled your cock from my mouth
like the pin to a handgrenade,
and what exploded was me,
pigeons' feathers, sequins,
these hundred-odd poems.
I feel like Charlie Chaplin
tightening up his belt in the soup line.
Without you I am such a puritan,
always just before the revolution.
You say all revolutions are circles
and disappear like a kite after
the string has broken,
swept away in new grace.

3.

The emptier a belly becomes
the wider it swells until
it looks like a beer belly
and you are pregnant with death.
It is the same with love,
After a while you have to laugh,
an hysterical pregnancy of sorts,
as you grow ugly, bloat with need.
Every time I see Kitty Carlisle
I think of you. The circle
is playing another tune.
I wish it was a waltz.
You can pretend to be lost in a waltz
but the music always circles home.

ROSA LUXEMBURG, DRAG QUEEN

As the curtain rises
I am standing in the middle of the stage.
Troops clamor forward from all sides
on black, sweating horses,
pointing their bayonets
at the audience
like phalluses as,
in the background,
Abba sings "Disco Queen"
only I am not dancing
because my legs are bound,
my hands are hitched behind my back,
I am blindfolded,
and a wad of cloth smeared with blood
is stuffed in my mouth
like a soft apple.
The audience hardly hears the music at all
because of the commotion
of the horses and troops
surrounding me.

The officer
commands me to sing the disco version
of "Bread and Roses"
so that the audience,
already swaying in their seats,
will have something to dance to
as a bayonet is slowly slipped
under my dress.
Castrated boys sing sweeter.
But, of course, because I am gagged
I can't sing,
I can't even move my lips to the words
which is the customary practice.
There are no recordings of Rosa Luxemburg
singing "Bread and Roses" in any version.
I would refuse to sing anyway.

My silence
becomes another kind of music,
and while the record is playing
and I am not moving my lips,
the audience knows
whose fantasy this is.
At this moment I am no longer a fantasy,
but the reality of the blood
of the people, their outrage and revolt.
Let the bullets sing for me.
I am no masochistic illusion.

Let the breath of Capitalism
choke on the blood that flows
from my new body,
a man without balls
in a soiled and torn dress
with sagging, punctured falsies
that have suddenly taken on
an aura of their own.
I am here,
not to entertain,
not to mimic,
but to die
as she died
in the German Revolution.

The soldiers stuff potatoes
under my dress
as if my asshole were an old sack.
They herd the glittery faggots
onto the stage
and shoot them,
then dump their bodies
like sacks of potatoes
into the backdrop
on which a dark river is painted.

The music stops.
Only the sound of gunfire
pricks the hot air
like the knife of a single, sadistic murderer
thrust into the same body
a hundred times.
The last bullet
is placed squarely
between my eyes.

I am no longer a man or woman,
a drag queen or a flimsy
imitation of Rosa Luxemburg.
I am the androgynous corpse.
My swollen body sings
without making a sound,
the sound all murdered faggots
and poor people and oppressed people everywhere make,
like the thud of a heavy hammer
as they dump us into the black, chaotic river
of history.
The music
that cannot be stopped begins,
the voice of innocent blood
rushing out of our bodies
into the river.

You see,
not all drag queens
are stage struck,
not all aspire
to become pop singers
or movie stars.
There are other reasons
why a man might choose
to dress in drag.

JAMES DEAN

for Harry Dean

> *"to move is to love"*
> —Frank O'Hara, from "James Dean"

I wanted James Dean
to take off all his clothes
and slowly lick me off
until I became the famous mist
that surrounded his eyes,
the visible mystery, why
people thought he was dreaming
or always on drugs
like a jazz musician
looking for high C
or someone who believes
in myths. Well,

you can't be a kid forever
and I looked pretty good once,
but I'll never look as good as
James Dean in *East of Eden*
when he shows his brother
the whorehouse, the truth.
We didn't have a whorehouse
on Bisvey Drive, we had Mary
Pottersfield. The guys used to drag
to the end of the dead-end street
where Mary lived
after her father was found dead
in his car, asphyxiated, at peace,
not like the mangled losers
in a quick game of chicken.
Mary turned bad, turned to
boys, all hoodlums, the kind
who'd murder their fathers,
with one thing on their minds.

We couldn't allow these guys to
sputter and backfire down
our quiet street with one thought
on their minds when that one
pure intention was
how to get into Mary's pants
which was the silent song
that accompanied the fathers
Saturday mornings
while they mowed the lawns
and Mary bounced down the street
on her way to the dance studio
in tight jeans with her
white blouse knotted limbo-rock
style around her waist,
breathing behind her enormous tits.
I knew my ideas about sex
were different. James Dean,
I cried in my pillow,
take *me* to the planetarium.
We can live in a house
by ourselves like the abandoned
mansion and live a moral life
without a cause. I wouldn't
even mind if you pretended
I was Natalie Wood though
I'd prefer to be Sal Mineo,
gangly and doomed, ready
to defend my hallucinations
with a gun. You wanted
to save him. You loved him.
He was a friend of yours.
I know that sounds
like pure rock and roll,
the cancer of music,
but these are strange times
and stranger cells find haven
in our bodies. We're the
mutants who appear for
appearances' sake,
as if life really were shallow,

callow, unconcerned with
the life you feel like you possess,
Buddhistic.
God is a cancer that
wants to eat your every
living thought, like the monk
who spoke only God's name
as if he could pick up the guy
when the guy was the most
beautiful creature in the bar.
James Dean, you are a teen-
age god, the wrecker
of the star system
because you had attitude,
were difficult to interview,
a beatific heart. You weren't
meat or celluloid.
You turned the word "star"
into "cypher," a permanent
memorial to the wisdom
of the rebellious child
who escaped brain damage
by dying young, an angel of
hallucinogenic masturbation.
James Dean, you are not
your father's dream of you.
If we don't love our fathers
but choose them as opponents,
we become true anti-heroes,
a modern gene
invented in France
during or shortly after
the Resistance.

* * *

I dated
a fat Jewish girl. She
convinced me to try to
fuck her. She waited until
the party ended. She
took off all her clothes.

I didn't want to touch her
knowing it would estrange us.
She was ugly and fat but
sincere. She pulled me into   .
her bed and
I couldn't get it up.
Later, I wrote a somewhat
romanticized poem about this
but the truth was,
I couldn't get James Dean
out of my mind. I wanted him
to get it up for me,
stick it deep into my asshole
and pump me
until we were beautiful,
glued together with semen and
ready to go again.
I will never go to bed
with anyone unless I think
exactly that.

Sex, especially wanton,
reckless sex, causes cancer.
It grabs your balls
and swings you like a rock
in Daniel's sling,
the one that struck Goliath
whose fall
penetrated the earth.
Then it eats out your heart
bite by bite
until you are heartless,
scornful and injured
but still alive, like Chiron,
but lacking wisdom.

James Dean, if you
are the anti-hero,
only you have the power
to make me the hero
who turns the energy of

his hurt upon the world,
and changes it. I'm sorry
you died in a sports car
accident. I guess if you'd
survived you'd have been
horribly scarred. But
even God couldn't face that,
so he took you
before your face hit the glass.
It was a miracle.

He always looked as if
he saw the golden city,
and it was safe
in the vulnerable arrogance
of his eyes. He was speech-
less, unable to betray it.
Unlike Rimbaud,
he didn't describe it
but he lived towards it
only mistaking
the alchemy of speed
for The Way. He believed
angels were invisible
because they were pure speed
and he wanted to see one
but who can say if he saw
the one sent to save him.
It may only have been
a sensation of the immortal,
what it means to be
remembered by the stars
one flashing second
before one has stopped desiring it.

CURING HOMOSEXUALITY

for three incurables, Frank, Stu and Richard

"There are no homosexuals, only fallen heterosexuals."
— Dr. Reuben Sebastian Wildchild

Of the many known and proven
cures for homosexuality,
the most familiar, perhaps,
is the Catholic Church's version of
"Confession-is-good-for-the-soul."
According to this ritual, every time
you feel an unclean urge to touch your-
self, you stop your hand with the
mental image of the Pope staring you
in the face and these words: "if-I-do-this-
I-have-to-tell-the-priest-again."
Then, when you go to confession you
enumerate and fully describe every such
forbidden act leaving out not the
slightest detail and the priest,
who lives anonymously in a dark box,
tells you what you must do to redeem your lost
soul. This usually amounts to kneeling
before a statue of this virgin
who has never allowed the sinful hands
of any man to ever infest her body
with the puerile desires of the flesh and
mutter a prayer that
you won't touch other men hail Mary as you,
in a religious rapture,
fondle your beads.
                    If this doesn't work,
and one wonders about these
good men whose career it is to sit in the dark
and listen to the pornography of everybody

else's life, the next step is psychoanalysis.
The doctor sits solemnly in the dark
behind you, his hands suspiciously folded
in his lap, and doesn't say a word
while you lie down on a long, lumpy sofa
and tell him about your childhood
and how much you hate yourself
for thinking the things you think
so uncontrollably
and you wish your tongue would fall out
and it almost does as you go on and on
wondering what the hell this fellow
is listening for as you start inventing
stories about Uncle's anus and house pets.
You soon find out he is interpreting
the things you tell him. According to
psychoanalytic theory, everything you say
means something else even more sinister
than what you meant. Your unknown desires
live within you and control your outward be-
havior. For instance, if you say,
"It's such a beautiful day today
I wanted to leave work early,"
the psychiatrist will interpret this to mean
you are dissatisfied with your job
and this in turn means you are sexually frus-
trated and this goes back to your miserable
childhood which means he'll probably
respond with, "Do you think that this means
you resented your mother when she
wouldn't let you play with yourself?"
If you say you had a dream about flying
he'll interpret it as a dream of sexual
frustration and penis envy meaning
you are really sick since only women
are supposed to have penis envy. He'll
probably ask you, "How did you feel when
you first saw your father's instrument?

Did you notice if it was bigger than yours?
Did he seem ashamed of his?
Did you want to touch it?"
If you tell him you don't recall
what it looked like he'll tell you
you unconsciously wanted it to fall off
so you could flush it down the toilet.
If you tell him you wanted to kill your father
and rape your mother he'll tell you
you had an Oedipus conflict.
He will listen for key words like
umbrella, closet, brother, rooster, shit, nude
amd Judy Garland, all of which convey
a large surplus of unconscious homo-
sexual material. For instance, never say:
"I put my umbrella in the closet
and found my brother in the backyard
beating the shit out of a rooster
while looking at nude pictures of
Judy Garland." To a psychiatrist this means:

umbrella = phallic symbol = womb = death = fear that it will rain at
    your funeral and no one will come
closet = phallic symbol = womb = mother = castration = desire to
    work for a fast food chain = prostitution = fear of underwear
brother = phallic symbol = sibling rivalry = castration = desire to
    stick your finger up your ass and smell it
rooster = phallic symbol = cock = flying = fear of Karen Black =
    crashing = fear of impotence = hatred of women = fear of oxygen
shit = phallic symbol = fear of dirt = work = puritan work ethic =
    father's penis = sexual frustration = deviations = fascination with
        dirt = bad toilet training = sexual hostility toward pilgrims
nude = phallic symbol = opposite sex = original sin = truth = fear of
    gardens = self-deception = poor sanitation habits = desire for
        death and return to Earth Mother = return to disco = hatred
            of mother = love of analyst but always waiting for some-
                one to come along and say no = desire to live in a
                    hole in the ground

Judy Garland = phallic symbol = fear of tornadoes = love/hate of
sucking = confusion of identity = desire to have oral relations with
a lap dog = necrophilia = fear of Easter bonnets = desire to
be a woman = fear of bad breath = spiritual destitu-
tion = desire to be Dr. Kinsey = existential mal-
function = fear of tubas = fear of dude ranches
and desire to perform unnatural acts with
Mickey Rooney = fear of short,
pimply people
Like a cancer, one sentence can devour your entire psyche.

If you say you had a hard time coming today
and you don't have anything to say
he'll call that resistance. If you say
it isn't, he'll say that's more resistance.
If you stop resisting, he'll call that
passive-aggressive. If you tell him
you've had it, you're tired of wasting
time and money when you haven't even begun
talking about homosexuality, he'll tell you
your problems run even deeper than he
initially realized and you need hospitalization.

Once you are hospitalized, the doctors
will begin electric shock therapy.
They call it therapy. There is no resistance.
You are not sure who's getting the therapy,
you or the sadistic maniacs who strap you down
and wire you up and turn on the juice
while they flash pictures of naked men
on a screen. The idea is to associate pain
and the fear of death by electrocution
with naked men. Then a comforting female
nurse unstraps you and wheels you, unconscious,
back to your room where she slowly
but surely revives you and stuffs a few pieces of
stale toast and cold eggs down your gullet.
This is supposed to turn you on to women.

none of these cures works
you will probably be thrown out of high school
as a bad influence for all those guys who
make you suck them off in the shower,
then beat you up at the bus stop. If you
still wish to remain homosexual, you will prob-
ably be arrested in the public library
for browsing too long in the "Sexuality"
section or during one of the periodic raids
of a local gay bar or face charges for soliciting
a cop who arrested you and forced you
to give him a blow job while he played
with his siren. In prison
you will probably be gang raped by
lusty straight men who are only acting out
their healthy but stifled heterosexual impulses
and if you are lucky one of them may even
win you in a knife fight and protect you
from the gang except when he trades you
out for a night for a pack of cigarettes or
a shot of heroin. Once you are released
you will become an expert in American
legal procedures as you face future charges
of child molestation, murder and attempts
to overthrow the common decency, whatever that is.
When you have had it, and decide to hijack
a jet and escape, you will discover the small
but important fact that no nation under god
or red offers asylum, political or otherwise,
to a plane full of pansies.
Your best bet is to fly over
the Bermuda Triangle and click
your little red pumps together whispering,
"There's no place like home, there's no
place like home."

In olden days
the main cure for homosexuality (then
often known simply as witchcraft) was
to tie the suspected faggot to a tiny seat
on the end of a long pole suspended
over boiling water. The suspected faggot was then
submerged for half an hour or until
he stopped struggling, whichever happened first.
If he was still alive when they lifted him
from the vat, they spread an oil slick over the water,
resubmerged the suspect and struck a match.
If he went up in smoke,
it meant he was a godless heathen faggot
who deserved to go up in smoke. If a choir
of angels emblazoned the sky and God,
humming the Hallelujah Chorus,
personally pissed out the flames dancing
around the suffocating faggot's body,
he was allowed to return home if he promised
to register four times daily with the local
police and never get his hair cut
in a place called a boutique.

                        So, you see,
liberalism has increasd the life expectancy
of fairies. That's because we've evolved
into the world's wittiest, best groomed
ballroom dancers. Everyone's into
the Queen's vernacular, pierced ears, disco
and poppers. So long as you seek your partner
after dark in the mountains of Montana
at least one hundred miles distant
from the nearest living heterosexual
and keep your meeting anonymous and
under fifteen minutes with no visible
body contact or non-contacting foreplay,
you could not conceivably, even by the

most homophobic, be considered
or accused homosexual by anyone but the most
adamantine and intolerant straight person.
Thanks to science it is now well known
that homosexuality is not transmitted by
tiny springing bugs or bats. We are not burned
at the stake (except during ceremonial
occasions of state for example only)
in the larger urban centers today
though we may still face a constant barrage
of misdemeanors (nastier than a case of crabs)
such as littering, (i.e.,
don't drop your hanky in a city park),
jaywalking (i.e., no matter how cute the
cop may be, don't wiggle your ass when
you buzz across Connecticut Avenue
during rush hour in the middle of the block
waving you-whoo, you-whoo to your color-
ful friends) and loitering (i.e., situated
under the romantic moon in an open
park after dark behind willowy shade trees
on your knees with a look of ecstasy
on your face as he creams into your eager mouth
is considered loitering among other things).
Simple precautions will save you
from a life of humiliation and
all those long blank spots on your résumé
that you have to explain as time
to get your head together or
extended vacation or time spent nursing
your mother back to health
when you were really fired for
turning on a fellow office employee.

In conclusion, there are no known cures
for homosexuality. Faggots have survived
Christianity, psychiatry, social ostracism, jail,

earth, air, wind and fire, as well as the pink
triangle and concentration camps. Nothing
can reckon with you if you can reckon with yourself.
The facts have been available for a long, long time:
where there are human beings, there are faggots.
We were around clubbing each other over the head
just like straight cave men. We were considered magical
by some people. We were considered mysterious.
We were obviously different but not always hated.
Hatred is always self-hatred.
Denial is always fear.
It's easier for THEM when
we hate ourselves,
FEAR OURSELVES.
I don't have to and
I WON'T.
None of us knows how he got here,
for what reason we are here or
why we are who we are.
It is not obvious
and a swish doesn't make me any more obvious
than the lack of one.
I am obvious
because I AM.

CUTE

I was never handsome, always cute. What I lack in good looks I make up for in personal hygiene. When you are cute and hygienic, they call you clean-cut. Unless you are argumentative. Then they call you cute but spoiled. I think of Rimbaud as the embodiment of the cute genius. If you are not only cute, but act as if you are cute, they call you cute but conceited. If you are cute and withdrawn, they call you cute but unapproachable. In other words, you are never simply cute. But if you are handsome, you are expected to be a little hard to get to know. Then you become a challenge. The cute one is always supposed to give in at the right moment. This is especially true when the one asking you to give in is handsome. Then you are supposed to melt. A cute person always melts when touched by a handsome person. This is considered proper cute etiquette. The cute person is in a constant prayerful state. He knows he won't be cute forever though a handsome person is always handsome. He looks even sexier with neatly trimmed grey sideburns. He never greys any place else unless it adds to his distinction. Handsome persons are always masculine and cute persons are always feminine. Handsome persons are always twenty-eight and cute persons are always eighteen. After forty a cute person usually looks used and a handsome person looks resourceful. As I said earlier, a cute person must always shine hygienically. A handsome person can rough it because roughing it enhances his masculinity. Handsome persons always get married. Cute people are always mistresses. Handsome persons are acutely intelligent. Cute persons without an imagination should be good at memorizing jokes. When a handsome person is rude, that's called style. When a cute person is rude, that is being temperamental and childish. A cute person, forever a child star, is not wanted around for very long because he reminds the handsome person that age is a real thing as the veneer of cuteness begins to sag under layers of crows feet, wrinkles and fat. The handsome person must never be reminded that he's going to get old, too. He's always on the prowl for someone even cuter than the cute person he's currently with. When he's got one arm around you and is staring bug-eyed across a crowded room, that's called setting a high standard. When a cute person is out with his handsome lover, he must bask in the charisma of handsomeness or risk being labeled flighty. There are worshippers and idols. There are stars and extras. There are XKE's and Volkswagens. There are privileges and conveniences. There are peacocks and parakeets. The world is not fair. There are the fair and the fading. There are cute and handsome.

Photo by Jeffrey Miller

Born in Dayton, Ohio, on December 2, 1946, Jim Everhard was reared in the Virginia suburbs of Washington, D.C. He served a four-year enlistment in the Navy from 1966 to 1970 and, following that, spent the next eleven years working on a B.A. in English literature from George Mason University. His poems have appeared in *Gay Sunshine, Fag Rag, Mouth of the Dragon, Hanging Loose, The Iowa Review, Epos, Painted Bride Quarterly, New: American and Canadian Poetry,* several anthologies, etc. He is currently deeply in love with an egg and is working on more writing every day.

Published in paperback; there is also a specially bound hardcover edition of 26 lettered and signed copies, each with an additional handwritten poem by the author.